W9-CFB-318

"*Marriage Can Be Fun*"

Jon K. Kardatzke, M.D.

Marriage Can Be Fun

Requests for information should be addressed to:

New Wings
211 N. 135th St. W.
Wichita, Kansas 67235

1-800-763-9946

Jacket Design by Bruce Plank
Jacket Illustration and Cartoons by Tim Ladwig
Author photograph by Kent Burnett
Special thanks for editorial assistance to Juanita Royer

ISBN 096433621-9

Printed in the United States of America

Published by New Wings
Wichita, Kansas

I gratefully dedicate this book to Lorna, my beautiful wife of 36 years. She has taught me and learned with me the many "pearls" found in this book on making marriage more fun. Her gentle kind spirit, unswerving love, and willingness to put up with and even participate with my wild and crazy antics added immensely to the many good times we have shared. She has helped me learn to listen, to be more expressive about love to my family, and to throttle my seemingly natural "bent" to be overcritical. What a beautiful person in every way!!

I love you lots, Babe!

"Here's my wallet, watch and fishing pole, and . . .,
Oh, I forgot my wife."

PROLOGUE

Do you want a fun-filled happy life? Do you want a super marriage, great sex, and to love and to be loved forever? Is gold gold? Are deer dear? Are sweets sweet? Is boring boring? Is exciting excitin'? Is fun fun? Yes, of course to all of the above! In this witty, but extremely practical book you will find many overlooked "pearls" that will add much joy and fulfillment to your marriage. It's true that 99.9% of marriages could succeed with enough work, play, knowledge, desire, and true grit. Are you willing to spend an hour or two to read, then re-read, then talk about what you just read in these 100 pages with your spouse? Try it. You'll like it. I double dog dare you!

Jon Kardatzke, M.D.

HOT TABLE OF COOL CONTENTS

ACT I

Marriage Can be Fun

"Hey, Buster, you're really starting to bug me."

Chapter 1

ARE WE HAVING FUN YET?

"*Y*ou're such a sour old grouch," Jackie said to Ken.

"Me?" he replied, "What about you? It's all your fault. What happened to the sweet, sexy girl that I married?"

"Listen you pot-bellied, balding dweeb," Jackie retorted. "If I treated you the way you treat me, you would have walked out years ago."

"You bleached-blonde old bag! Are you suggesting divorce?"

"If that's what you want, you spider sucking lizard!"

Would you say that the *romance* has *possibly* gone out of Ken and Jackie's marriage? Unluckily, their situation is all too common. Did you know that most marriages end because of illness? The husband and wife get *sick of each other!* What happens to more than three-fourths of marriages to cause the romance, love, and the old "zing!" to die out? With divorce rates at fifty percent and another twenty-five percent of marriages just barely existing together, is there any real hope for marriage at all? Has God's plan flopped? Why do so many marriages fail, even among Christian couples? Most experts agree that the answer is found in several key points:

1) Lack of commitment
2) Unrealistic expectations
3) Inadequate preparation for married life
4) Lousy communication
5) Forgetting to play

Let's take a moment to look at each of these five points on which we will elaborate later in the book.

1. Lack Of Commitment

Free Love! Follow your fantasy! If it feels good, do it! Do you recognize any of these slogans? The 1960's introduced America into a self-oriented, feel good mentality that has invaded the minds of millions of red-blooded Americans ever since. A new slogan introduced in the 1990's screams at us to "Just Do It!" What happens when we take this slogan seriously and "do it" (get married) then wish we hadn't? Or what do we do when the newness wears off, or when fantasy and elation fade into reality?

Very often marriage quickly changes from a state of BLISS to a state of MISS, from BLESSED to MESSED, but always marriage quickly enters a state of transition, the "period of adjustment" (which actually continues till death doth you part). This early adjustment period is essential and must occur successfully for a happy marriage to result. We must adjust to many things: cold eggs, hot ice cream, his dirty shorts slung on your pillow, wet panty hose dripping on your back in the bath tub, morning breath, evening gas, Monday A.M. blues, monthly visits from "the curse," paying the rent, utility bills, doctor bills, irritability, headaches, not "in the mood." He stops closing the door when using the bathroom. She stuffs his snoring mouth with his dirty sweat socks. Then we find out quickly that commitment is far more than a feel-good feeling. Do we *have* to adjust to these things? A growing love may involve *correcting* some of them. Part of adjustment is learning to change some habits that are offensive to our mate. Love is never free. Neither does loving someone always feel good. As Gary Smalley makes clear in his video: "Love is not a feeling. Love is a decision."

2. Unrealistic Expectations

Did you marry Mr. or Mrs. Right? Did you find the perfect mate? Of course not! Are *you* the perfect mate? Of course not! God has never created such an animal. There is no true love waiting for your eyes to lock with his when you just happen to walk into some dimly lit room somewhere. (With my face, the dimmer the better!) Yet, at first we all expect too much from marriage, and disillusionment soon follows. I remember dreaming of my future bride who would be soft and sweet, beautiful, sexy, outgoing, quiet, demure, feminine, athletic, tall, short, blonde, brunette, fair complected, deeply tanned, always happy, etc. See any contradictions and unrealistic expectations? No matter what Hollywood tries to tell us, real love doesn't happen in one romantic glance. So turn off the TV and learn how to be a star in your own romantic love story. Discover the lover who conveniently already lives in your own home.

Once upon a time there was a kind and beautiful princess who fell in love with a very handsome prince. Within a short time, the handsome prince whisked the princess off her feet to the never-never land of married bliss. No one told the prince or the princess that the castle they were to inherit had a huge mortgage on it, a leaky basement, a few rodents, and foundation problems. Before they were married the kind and beautiful princess forgot to warn the prince that once a month for about five days she turned into a short-tempered, sour, wild woman. (In those days, no one had ever heard of PMS.) The prince forgot to warn the princess that he sometimes would forget to bathe for days, had the habit of picking his toes before making love and always left the castle toilet seat up. What do you suppose happened to the starry-eyed romance between the handsome prince and the beautiful princess? Most of us would guess that the fire fizzled fast, that the princess and prince wanted out of their "fairy-tale" romance. What ever happened to "happily-ever-after?"

"Elmo claims it's a horror flick.
They end up getting married."

3. Inadequate Preparation For Married Life

How many of us have ever read a book about marriage or have attended a marriage seminar? Fewer than 3%. Most of us have spent far more time reading about Hollywood's "changing partners" scene than we have in learning how to be a better marriage partner ourselves. No wonder we don't understand the complexities and responsibilities of marriage. We just know that "we're in love!"

What happens when the Cinderella story has turned to cinders? What happens when the handsome prince turns out to be a toad in disguise? What happens when the beautiful princess you married turns into a wicked witch? If you have asked any of these questions then you can be positively sure that you have successfully passed through the infatuation stage! Congratulations! Now it's time to get to work. Learn to work hard at pleasing your mate and at developing common interests. Study together about relationships, love, etc.

4. Lousy Communication

How many wars could have been avoided with better understanding between nations? How many millions of broken marriages could have been saved from the divorce court through learning and applying skills of communication? We will communicate about communication very communicably in Act VI!

5. Forgetting To Play

Most successful marriages I have seen are those in which FUN has been a big part of the relationship. Good times, frivolity, laughter, fun teasing and good sex will unite a couple more than almost any other factors. Learn to PLAY TOGETHER! You're still just kids, even at SEVENTY!

Is there any chance for the institution of marriage? Is there any hope for your marriage? YES! A *resounding* YES! Marriage can be fun again if you want it to be and are willing to learn to commit, to work, and to play. However, it will take a conscious and unconscious effort, a willingness to forgive and to ask for forgiveness, and a re-commitment to trying to please your mate unselfishly. "What can I do to make her (him) happier?" This book is different from any ever written about marriage and will give you a new lease on life together if you will apply what you read to your marriage.

MARRIAGE CAN BE FUN!

Let's set the stage for the party!

1. What does commitment mean to you?

2. What unrealistic expectations did you have coming into your marriage?

3. Why have so few couples attended a marriage seminar or even read one book about marriage?

"My marriage would be perfect – without Elmo."

Chapter 2

LOVE – INSTANT OR CONSTANT?

The following is a short story that unfortunately happens all too often in real life:

"Last fall I went to a dance with my fiancee. As we entered the hall, I saw this unbelievable vision of beauty and charm across a crowded room and our eyes locked instantly. Staring at me longingly, she left her date, did a pivot turn, and glided sensuously across the room in her five inch spike heels, her long blond hair glistening in the strobe lighting. I ran forward eagerly and swept her into my strong sinuous arms and our mouths met devouring each other in a timeless moment of romantic ecstasy. It was truly love at first sight. We were married the next day and enjoyed happiness and bliss forever after. Unfortunately three weeks later, the witch left me."

Love at first sight sounds so romantic, but what is much more romantic *is love after 30 years of seeing each other.* Now that's TRUE LOVE. Most true love *begins* with infatuation. "She makes me so happy." "I am so excited to be near him." As teens, we often fantasize about how wonderfully our spouse will treat us, how she will *always* be beautiful, kind, unselfish, serving our every need. But as our love matures into true love and a lasting commitment, we must learn to turn this around. i.e. How can I make her happy? What can I do for him? As we learn to grow deeper and deeper in love, we should remind ourselves often in the first fifty years of marriage of the many good qualities we saw in each other early on. What did I like about him? Why did I marry her? List these mentally or write them down. As the scripture says "think on these things."

11

Fix on the positive. Hang the negative. Your spouse has many more pluses than minuses or you wouldn't have married. Is he gentle, considerate, witty (at least half way)? Is she a good listener, a good cook, a great talker, a caring Mom? Is he a good provider, a loving Dad, and fun to be with? Does she say yes more than no? Does he? Do her cold feet wake you up in time for work? Does he provide sonorous soothing music in his sleep? Certainly there are many more things you can think of that are good traits about your spouse. "Think on these things" again and again!

True love then is a choice. It is commitment, faithfulness in bad and good times, honoring and preferring one another. It's awesome to be in AWE of your spouse after thirty years. Try it — say it — "I awe you."

"I AWE YOU — I LOVE YOU!"

1. List differences in true love versus infatuation.

2. Is true love perfection?

3. Does true love need to be spoken?

"Elmo finally brought Magic to our relationship –
he vanished."

Chapter 3

FOR BETTER OR WORSE!

For most people, marriage can be the best way to live a contented, happy, love-filled life, or the worst! Many of us felt that we couldn't be happy without marriage and family. On the other hand, many of you may have felt at one time or another that you should have taken the apostle Paul's advice and remained single. (Romans 7)

Would you really have been happier? Just look at the rut you're in! If your life is like most of us, you probably still don't own a Corvette. You have a house full of bratty kids. (Paternal cause: New studies show that mis-behavior is passed on only through the male gene!) You may have big debts, a critical non-loving slob of a husband, a nagging wife, etc....etc....etc.... With so many problems in marriage, it's easy to understand how married people can fall into the trap of fantasizing.

> "Oh, how wonderful and simple life would have been if I hadn't gotten hitched!"

Well folks, it ain't true!! Single or married, we'll all have problems and if you don't believe that the loneliness of single life can be tough, too, just ask someone who is single. Good marriages are not "made in heaven" as much as they are *built* with hard work here on earth, and most bad marriages can be good ones with enough work, communication, and commitment. Although all marriages have problems, the potential for learning and applying the principles of God's love is very great indeed when two people commit and submit themselves to each other as taught in the Scriptures.

Submit to one another out of reverence to Christ.
Esphesians 5:21

*Each one of you also must love his wife as he loves himself
and the wife must respect her husband.*
Esphesians 5:21

*. . . at the beginning of Creation God made them male and
female. For this reason a man will leave his father and
mother and be united to his wife, and the two will become
one flesh. So they are no longer two, but one; therefore what
God has joined together let man not separate.*
Mark 10:6-9

IT'S NOT TOO LATE. Your marriage can be fun too! Just
the fact that you are reading this book gives you a far better
than average chance of a happy marriage because you are
seeking. Most couples never bother. So you've already got a
head start and it will get "funner!"

In this book we will discuss love, problem solving, keeping the "Zing!" in marriage, sex, commitment, family
finances, and communication. We will talk about ways to
make your marriage happier, to make it more fun to live
together. We will occasionally drop on you a number of
"pearls" that will contain GREAT WISDOM!

Pearl #1: There are two key principles in learning to understand women — but nobody knows what they are!

1. Why did you decide to marry rather than to remain single?

2. Is it really possible to still have fun together after 25 years?

3. If the "thrill is gone," can it be restored?

4. What can you do, starting today, to put the fun back in your marriage?

"You'll never find a man if you
set your standards too high."

Chapter 4

WHY HIM, WHY HER???

*N*ow, I want to ask you to reflect back on your pre-marriage years, (the good old days?) and try to remember what you wanted out of your future marriage. What were the main hopes and goals that you thought marriage would help you achieve?

Riches	Escape
Security	Companionship
Love	Family-Children
Sex	Happiness
Romance	?????????

Was it great the first day or did things go wrong even on day one of your wedding and/or honeymoon? The night Lorna and I got married our car wouldn't start. She cried because on the three hour drive to the hotel she realized she had left home for good (maybe), and by the time we arrived at midnight in Honeymoon Heaven we were both "too tired." (But at three AM we found energy anew!) When our first daughter Teri married, she and her husband spent the first 48 hours with only one hour of sleep, 24 hours of travel, 8 hours of stomach flu, and 10 minutes of "marital bliss." What a romantic start!

Do you realize that the same two people in a marriage can either be miserable or happy? It is a matter of choice, of work, of sacrifice, of commitment, and a lot of applied love. Each of us couples has a choice — happiness together or misery together. Which do you choose?

Now, let's build our foundation for a better marriage by re-examining why you chose to marry Sir Lancelot or Honey Buns. (Maybe you now call him or her "the jerk," or "the old bag"!) Out of all the billions of people on this planet, why him, why her? What things did you like about her or him that made you decide to spend fifty years together? What factors made you choose this one?

Looks — (When Lorna chose me this must have been a strong factor!)

Personality Traits — pleasant, fun, someone you felt comfortable with or enjoyed talking with, someone opposite to yourself, someone kind, gentle, considerate, and sympathetic.

Intelligence

Financial security

Common interests

Sex — attitudes or just plain sexy

Religious beliefs

The only person you could find who would marry you?

I'm sure there were many things you liked about each other the day you decided to "get hitched," but all too often as the newness wears off after marriage, romance shrivels, fights begin, and you decide you no longer are "in love." What causes the hope of two young lovers to die in divorce or misery?

Did you really love him or her right at first? Was it true love at first sight? No, true love takes time to mature. So then, what is the difference between true love and infatuation?

THE CRITERIA OF TRUE LOVE
Devotion and commitment
Liking each other
Choosing to love each other even when you don't like
  each other
Lasting
Constant nourishment
Being other person oriented – conscious, empathetic,
  caring

INFATUATION — (It was fascination, I know!)
Short lived
Intense
More emotionally extreme — especially high
Fickle
Self oriented – pathetic, uncaring

Infatuation asks: "How can she make me happy?" — **GET**
True love asks: "How can I make her happy?" — **GIVE**

Hopefully you have a good measure of true love developing in your marriage relationship, and, remember, you can *grow* in your love relationship if you are willing to try. If you feel the fire of love is dying, it can be rekindled. Everyone has problems in marriage relationships but there is hope!

"Don't forget, you wouldn't even have been born if
I had been the *least* bit choosy."

1. Why did you marry your spouse? What were his/her good traits that attracted you?

2. Can true love really die?

ACT II

Romancing Can be Fun

"Elmo always has a big party on our anniversary.
Just once I wish he would invite me."

Chapter 5

LET'S PLAY

How can you keep the fun in your marriage or put fun back into a relationship that has gone sour? Has your marriage grown so stodgy, dull, and boring that fun is just a three letter meaningless word? Have anger and resentment been allowed to smolder so long that you can't laugh together, can't remember the good times that you used to have? Can a sick, lifeless marriage be restored back to health and life and FUN again?

Even after the honeymoon is over, as we settle into a routine, as we adjust, CAN MARRIAGE BE FUN????? REALLY??? HOW???

1) By being the best of friends. Be interested in each other. Do you know your spouses likes, dislikes, favorite things, childhood experiences, present desires, ambitions?

2) By having a good sense of humor. Learn how to laugh again. You don't have to be a "stuffed shirt" even if you are by nature quiet and reserved.

3) Never lose the kid in you! Enjoy life. Set traditions (Christmas tree, pumpkins, hunting, rattlesnake roundups, (Send mate to be the forward spotter and snake pit tester), camping...(You've never lived until you take a family camping trip!) Be a *little* crazy, maybe *a lot.* (Sure is easy for me.)

4) Lighten up – Get down and boogie. Learn how to be playful again.

5) Learn to tease and joke with sensitivity. No jokes about weight or intelligence please.

6) Be willing to do some things for the pleasure of your mate. Fishing, snipe hunting, bowling, shopping with her, watching him or her play baseball. Play basketball with him (but let him win!!)

7) Learn to enjoy good sex (with your mate only). What fun!!

8) Go out together frequently. Second honeymoons x2000 (see next chapter).

9) Have a fun relationship with your kids. Don't forget you'll only have them with you for a few years.

10) Sing together. Laugh together. (When I sing, we all laugh!)

11) Look for ways to please each other. Surprises are nice.

12) Look good to one another. Smell good to one another.

13) Be good to one another.

14) Forgive and forget.

15) Ask God for help in restoring the good times in your relationship.

1. Can fun and games be put back into a stale, boring, or hostile marriage?

2. Can you think of more ways to play and have fun?

3. Are smiling and laughing infectious diseases?

"I haven't told you that I love you recently,
but I almost thought it once!"

Chapter 6

FOR A GOODER BOND

*N*ow, what are some areas of your marriage relationship that you would like to improve? To make your marriage more fun, what would need to change? How many of these would give new zest to your marriage?

1) More displays of affection: (Kisses, squeezes, loving pat, love expressions).
2) Less Yelling.
3) More mutual respect.
4) More time together, quality and quantity.
5) More common goals and interests.
6) More helping each other. (Are you a help-mate?)
7) More attention to physical fitness.
8) More dough, less debt.

Now, WHO should do all the changing? Your spouse, of course! No, seriously. YOU must change if you want your mate to change. Find out or ask yourself what she or he would like to see you do that would make your relationship better. Ask yourself, "How can I start the process of healing? Can I be kinder, more interested in him or her, more interested in my own appearance? Can I laugh more, be brighter, and be less angry, less hostile, or less depressed?"

Now that you have examined what changes you can make, ask yourself, "How can we change our relationship?" In most cases you will find that if you change, you relationship will change for the better or worse, depending on how you change. So, these are your first assignments to begin right away:

#1. Ask each other what are two things that you would like to see change in each other or in your relationship to make you both happier and to increase the fun in your marriage?

#2. Wear something in the evening your mate really likes. Put on heels, fresh lipstick, black pantyhose and favorite perfume. (If she likes the way you look, you're both very sick!!!)

#3. Compliment each other once a day (even if it causes your brain to overheat or strains you so much you pop a hernia!)

#4. Tell your spouse "I love you" this week even if it sounds strange because it has been so long.

#5. Say something nice about his or her sexual prowess or sexiness. Example: Ask her to come put her curvy little behind on your lap. Now, wife, while sitting there, wiggle a little and then feed his male ego by asking him, "Is that a rock in your pocket or are you just glad to see me?"

#6. Try being playful with each other. Pretend it's your third date as you sit together on the couch.

#7. Look for ways you can help each other. Examples: Cleaning up the kitchen, laying out his clothes for tomorrow, helping more with kiddos, etc...

Remember, in order for a marriage to be successful, it requires a great deal of hard work, sacrifice, adjustments, commitment, and applied love as we share this life together. It can be fun if we learn to build on the all-important goal, a good husband-wife relationship.

1. What areas of your marriage need the most attention?

2. How can you help your mate enjoy your marriage relationship more?

"Hey – A night out is a great idea. Don't hurry back."

Chapter 7

MATE DATE

*D*o you remember your first date? Wasn't it fun? It probably was even exciting. Were you innovative as you continued dating or did you always go to Hot Dog Castle, get gas, and watch football on her parents' TV?? I'll bet you went to movies, played mini golf, watched airplanes take off, kissed in the moonlight over the lake, ate hot fudge sundaes together, threw snowballs, and lots of other silly stuff you're too grown up (or too lazy and boring) to do now.

Where did all the fun go? I know many married couples who never go out together, even for one evening, let alone spend a week together vacationing. What a mistake — what a bonehead move. (That's a medical term.) No wonder life seems dull and your marriage gets in a rut. This is all too common and entirely unnecessary, but it is easily remedied. So get with it!! You can afford it. Thirty bucks can buy plenty of food and entertainment for an evening and you both deserve it. It's so invigorating to get a break from the routine and from the kids even for three or four hours. It's also romantic! And now you're ready to try a whole night out! Let's really get foolish and spend one hundred dollars for a dinner date, a movie, and then a motel with a king size bed. Wow, how romantic, how sexy! Talk about bonding! You get to stay out late and everything, and then wind up in a motel, which can be erotic since you were not to do "that" before you were married.

What a turn-on! What a love match this can be. Even a family vacation to Colorado can be great fun, but be sure your bedroom is sound proofed and has a lock on the door!

Now, I dare you to be different on these dates. Maybe a call from the office to your sweety-pie (Clue-your wife) to make the date. Keeping romance alive for 50 years is achievable, but IT TAKES WORK AND PLAY!

Tenderness, love, touching, frequent love expression, praising, and affirmation are all key ingredients to a forever kind of romance. Women love cards and small gifts (occasionally a large one.) Men love pats on the behind, a sexy greeting. Women like back rubs; men like front rubs. We all love to be told "You are the best. I'm glad I married you." Helping each other in daily tasks, spending time with your children together, renting a romantic video, etc. Tell her she's a foxy babe. Tell him he's YOUR MAN, (especially when he wears an apron to help you with the dishes). AND DON'T FORGET THE FLOWERS! Don't wait until she dies, guys. A $5.00 small assortment is a thrill to our wives. If you're really a super cheapo you can get them free from a funeral home like someone I know. Also surprises can be great. Can you think of any? Maybe one??

So get with it, "DUDE." Have a great mate date!!!

1. List five things that you would really enjoy doing together.

2. Why is sex so much fun in a motel?

3. Do you fully understand the value of just the two of you getting away without the kids fairly often?

"Tonight we must eat and run. I lost my billfold."

Chapter 8

10 KEYS TO A FUN MARRIAGE

*T*o summarize then, the following 10 "Biggees" will give great strength to your renewal efforts in restoring or increasing the good times in your marriage.

1) **Communication.**
   Talk often. Listen. Tackle problems. Avoid walls. Share feelings. Express love.

2) **Keep Fit.**
   - Feel good.
     Good nutrition, regular exercise, stop smoking.
   - Look good.
     Weight control, proper cosmetics, hair care.
   - Smell good.
     Soap, deodorants, colognes.

3) **Keep Romance Alive.**
   Be kind and thoughtful. Also send loving notes and cards. Flowers are special. Practice the three organic ways of kissing: Peaches, Prunes, and Alfalfa. Use pet names: "Sweetie, Honey-pot, My man, Big Hunk." Whisper sweet somethings in his/her ear often. "You're so sexy. You're my lover. You turn me on. You're so beautiful." See the chapter on mate date.

4) **Learn To Be Nice To Mate.**
   Compliment. Respect opinion. Do nice things for each other. Treat your mate better than you would your best friend. Make your spouse your best friend. Be considerate, soft spoken, understanding. Can you follow the golden rule with your mate? Remember the golden rule: "Do unto others as you would have others do unto you."

5) **Be Fun.**
   Learn to laugh. Act a bit stupid just for fun. Make each other laugh. Tease with sensitivity. Take fun trips together. Never lose the "Kid" in you.

6) **Avoid Financial Worries.**
   Don't buy on credit. Interest can bury you. Budget your income and outgo. Buy wisely.

7) **Good Sex Relationship.**
   Variety is important to both of you (more later). Knowledge — read. We can all learn more about sex. Sensitivity to mate's needs and desires.

8) **Commitment.**
   This is vital to all other areas of our marriage relationship. Be trustworthy and true to your mate. Put your marriage above all other human relationships.

9) **Keep a Positive Attitude.**
   You can make it with God's help. Marriage can be great.

10) **Keep A Relationship Perspective.**
    I. You and God
    II. You and your Mate
    III. You and Children
    IV. You and Others

"I know its clam chowder.
I can almost chew the shells."

God did not plan for divorce. He wants us to be happy together, to have fun together, to probe, explore and discover the true meanings of love in the closest and deepest human relationship possible — MARRIAGE.

MISSION POSSIBLE — YOUR MARRIAGE CAN BE FUN!

Pearl #2: If your mate were absolutely perfect, she/he sure wouldn't have picked you! Because you are imperfect too!

1. Does God want your marriage to be competing or completing? Why?

2. Is romance possible after 10 years?? How can we build on this?

3. Do you see the extreme importance of keeping your priorities in perspective? (Re-read #10)

ACT III

Sex Can be Fun

"Once a king, always a king–
but once a knight is enough."

Chapter 9

SEX FOR LIFE

an sex still be fun after five years? After ten years? Twenty? Thirty? With one spouse for life? Yes! Yes! Yes! But it takes work, willingness, and a strong desire to make each other happy in this extremely important area of marriage. I have known marriages in which the wife had not experienced orgasm in thirty years. I have counseled with many couples who have sex less than once a month, some once a year.

This may work for a rare couple, but in every situation of which I am aware at least one of the spouses is unhappy about this state of affairs. So, if sex is so important to a close relationship, and it is, can we make it more appealing again? How do we?

1) **Realize that the grass is really browner**. We all have heard the old adage "the grass is greener" meaning that the things you don't possess seem to look more appealing than the things you do! How does this apply to marriage? Many look at their mate during the bad times with doubt and wonder. "What if I had married 'the hunk' or what if I had married that sexy chick I dated?" Life would have been perfect. He wouldn't have had body odor. She would never have a headache and would always be alluring. Day dreams and fantasies can worm their way into our brains and can make our marriages seem dull.

Well folks, it's all a mirage. If you had married the other one, you would have at least as many problems as you do now, probably more! The other guy not only has B.O., but picks his nose in public. That other sexy "doll" has just as many hidden defects as your wife does and isn't nearly as loving and good with children as your wife is.

There is no perfect mate, no perfect life, no perfect children, and no perfect marriage. So quit the useless day dreams and get on with making your mate happier. You chose him or her for many good reasons. Remember these and think about them often!

You made a good choice. Work with the relationship you have and make it better.

The grass on the other side is not greener. It is really browner. Don't let this age old illusion make you discontent, flitting from one "pasture" to another. All green grass needs to be fertilized and mowed. So get to fertilizing. You are full of it, you know! (medical reference #5.) True happiness and new excitement can be the result of a new understanding of how lucky you are already. So, down with fantasy and up with reality! And you know what else! It's lots more fun!!

2) **Be more open with each another.** Great or even moderately good sex depends on love, security, and increasing intimacy in many areas of marriage. If problems of communication, emotion, anger, or trust arise, they must be tackled or your marriage bond will suffer. If unresolved, these issues will almost inevitably dampen your sexual fun times.

"Don't worry. There is no way
you could ever be a sex object."

3) **Be willing to learn.** Lorna and I are still learning new "funsies" after 36 years of marriage. Because of testosterone, men tend to be more aggressive and explorative about sex than women. But REAL men can help their wives to enjoy many of the wonderful more erotic forms of sexual pleasure by being patient, encouraging and complimenting. Over the years, you will be surprised and thrilled at the "tigress" you have unleashed in your wife. Of course in some couples the reverse of the above is true, but in many cases the wife is the partner who will be more reluctant to explore and diversify. By being patient, trustworthy, loving, and romantic, and by having honest communication about sex, we can all learn <u>from</u> our spouse new intimacies <u>with</u> our spouse.

4) **Keep physically fit.** Look, feel, and smell good to your mate. Can you do this? It is important? Ask your spouse. "Letting yourself go" often is a symptom of deeper emotional or physical problems and you may need to seek professional help.

1. Why is keeping physically, mentally, and emotionally fit so important? Why can't I just say "If you really love me, you'll accept me just the way that I am?"

2. How can I tell my mate my strongest and most intimate desires? I'm afraid he'll laugh or that she'll get angry.

"Hey big boy. Do I still turn you on?""

Chapter 10

SURPRISE: WE AIN'T THE SAME!

*A*ssuming that you both want a better conjugal bond with more and "gooder" sex and that you are both willing to learn, to explore, and to give more pleasure to your mate, let's get to the really good stuff!

Most of us know by now the illustration of a man's sexual responsiveness compared to a microwave oven and a woman's responsiveness to a crock pot. There is much truth in this and this knowledge can be used to advantage. For instance, a husband by prolonging foreplay etc., can enjoy much more pleasure and a more intense climax while his wife now can relax and enjoy the "warm up" time she is designed for to experience orgasm.

Many men and women alike have never understood that the clitoris is the same organ as the penis, just smaller and slower to become erect. It must be stimulated one way or another for full female orgasm. The "G-spot" is a lot tougher to find, let alone stimulate. Also, men must learn what "turns a woman on" and what doesn't. For instance, wifey can put on something sexy like heels and a hot outfit (topless, bottomless, frontless, backless) and our "favorite muscle" is instantly at attention. But we husbands can "bounce" out of the bathroom naked, jump around, pose, strut, flutter our eyelashes, flex our muscles, stick out our behinds, and what is our wife's response — uncontrollable laughter. So how do we turn on a crock pot? Most women say good sex at night begins in the morning. Fix her a cup of coffee. (Try not to burn the water!) Kiss her warmly (after you brush your teeth). Say "I love you" as you leave for work. Call her from work and tell her you are thinking about her and it's getting hard — to stay at work. When you come

53

home help her with the kids, with the dishes, (yes, that's true machismo), hug her four times, then secretly give her a love pat just out of the kids eyesight, and tell her she is beautiful.

What a beginning, but just a beginning. After you help her get the kids to bed, run her bath water, (take one yourself, too) shave, put on deodorant, hug her again twice, throw the dice, now you're ready for something nice! *IF* you do this regularly, it won't be such a shock, and your bonding will cement every time you show your love.

Now, a word to the wise — the wives! Since men are built by God to react quickly to the external, it is important that you also often look your best just for your husband. Greet him in the evening with fresh makeup, lipstick, favorite outfits, sometimes even high heels. Keeping yourself fit, flirting with him, etc., will do wonders for his vision! "Shake your bootie" and pop his eyes!

1. If my spouse wants more and better sex, do I have to enjoy it or can I just ask him to turn me over when he's through?

2. Should both of us enjoy sex to the max every time?

3. If my mate is not interested very often, what can I do?

"Hey big boy – How's about a *fun* new sexy game?
Think of your wildest, hottest fantasy!
You name it – and I'll try to spell it."

Chapter 11

SEXY SEX

"Sex is so much fun with you. I wish we could do this 24 hours a day!" said a young man to his bride of 6 weeks. Wouldn't it be wonderful if this excitement and energy could be in our marital relationships forever? Well, there are a few other things we need to do in life but probably none as full of fun and pleasure. So, read on and maybe we can help this terrific bonding enterprise!

Now, there are many books that give good insight into the mechanics of sexual techniques. You can find these in your nearest Christian or secular book store. But there are several key points I want to cover in this chapter.

- Sex in marriage can and should be sexier than secret encounters outside of marriage — even more exciting. Why? Because of the security in the good marriage relationship, the intimacy that is developed, and the turn-on principles and "inventions" a couple learns over the years. The desire of a spouse to give pleasures as well as receive, and the willingness to extend mutual pleasure and fun through new, yes, even erotic techniques and explorations together.

- Don't forget God created sex and there is nothing wrong or sinful about any sexual innovation and/or stimulating technique or position as long as it involves only the two of you, and doesn't cause physical or emotional pain or injury. However, chandelier swinging, sex on a bunje jump, erotic videos, bondage, etc. can be physically and mentally dangerous. There are so many positions and variations of intercourse and foreplay that you will be able to discover new delights for at least fifty years.

57

- Sensual body caresses can be very exciting to both husband and wife. It may take years of intimacy and love to fully progress to this in your sexual bonding so husbands encourage and be patient, and wives don't be afraid to learn. You can derive a lot of pleasure from this very sexy intimacy builder. Also, husbands must be willing to give as well as receive, if you get my drift. If you don't, you're not as sexy as you think you are!

- Baths, a good shave, deodorants, toothpaste, perfumes, and patience are all vital ingredients in love-making. Exotic skimpy outfits, high heels, and long earrings, black panty hose, hot lipstick, and even wigs can be very stimulating. But if your wife can't stop laughing when you wear these, ask her to try them! If she likes you in this getup – you're *both sick*!!

- One biggee I want to mention is "Don't forget the lube tube." Very few couples have discovered, even after 20 years of marriage, the importance of lubrication. The quicker we macho guys quit thinking that to prove our manhood and her womanhood we have to get her to be naturally moist, the quicker we can get on to better and hotter sex. Consider K-Y Jelly, hand lotions, whipping cream, body oils, flavored gels, chocolate syrup, and chicken soup.

- Variety is the spice of sex. This means:
  1. Positions
  2. Foreplay techniques
  3. Vibrators carefully used
  4. Time of day (not always late at night)
  5. Clothing
  6. Mirrors
  7. Place of encounters (Motels, fireplace, hammocks, kitchen table, refrigerator, etc. — Restaurants are out!)

As you "double your marital pleasure" with this very wonderful gift from God, you will notice temptations to stray to be much less alluring. After all, if you have "alluring gourmet desserts" at home, why go out for stale tapioca? If you have a hot potato at home, why go out for cold hash browns? Don't forget romance and music, and never, never, never forget a lock on your bedroom door!

1. If my spouse won't agree to variety in sex, should I leave?

2. Are any positions and turn-ons dangerous?

3. Is once a year enough? More often? Are you serious?

4. What can I do tonight to make our sex life come alive?

"How dare you say the thrill is gone!"

Chapter 12

THE MARRIAGE WRECKER

Since so many marriages, (way above 50%), are damaged or broken by an outside sexual affair, I am convinced that we should all become more aware of the ease in which we can become enmeshed. Whether we have a great marriage with super sex or not, we are all still potentially vulnerable to the awful curse of infidelity. Sex urges are very strong as is the desire for love and being loved. Even though you may think you are "above temptation," you are (like the rest of us) all too human! Even you pastors and deacons are susceptible, believe it or not! Of course women would never stoop to adultery? Ha! Who do we think the men are with—a rock??—perhaps a porcupine?? Now, how do we remain faithful for 50 years? Can we? YES!!

Avoiding Extramarital Entrapment
1. Have a good husband-wife relationship.
2. Value your family. Would you hurt your kids?
3. Live close to God in your daily experience.
4. Have fun sex with your spouse.
5. Please your spouse in many ways:
    Keep physically fit.
    Beautify yourself.
    Wear clothes your spouse likes.
    Frequently express your love and praise your spouse.
    Give positive strokes.
6. Turn away from temptation quickly! RUN AWAY! FAST! Don't play with fire.
7. Hugs and kisses with others should be discrete and proper. Side hugs and watch your hands!

8. No private "marriage counseling" with opposite sex unless with a professional marriage counselor.

9. Women, know that men look at "friendly flirtations" differently.

10. Recognize and understand our sexual vulnerability and sometimes "raging hormones."

11. Avoid alcohol, late hours, extended solo business trips.

12. Avoid excessive compliments to other sex (except to your spouse!)

13. Avoid pornography – UNREALISTIC FANTASY.

14. Seek counseling early if temptation or attraction towards someone begins to be a problem. TRUISM: FATAL ATTRACTION IS OFTEN EXACTLY THAT!!!

Don't forget this axiom:

Temptation says:
"Look at what you don't have — GO FOR IT."

God's wisdom says:
"Look at what you already have. Work hard to keep it."

1. What would you do first if you noticed more than a shallow attraction for another man or woman?

2. Does God care about this? How do you know? How can God help us to avoid the deadly traps of infidelity?

3. If I was unfaithful five years ago, should I confess to my spouse? Be cautious with this question! Most often the answer is no, but not in every situation. Use wisdom.

ACT IV

Yes, Even Feuding Can be Fun

"Why can't I ever call you a stupid ugly fathead
without you starting an argument?"

Chapter 13

DUEL OR DUET

rouble, double trouble, and triple trouble. Sound like your life at times? When you have problems that affect your marriage does it discourage you or make you feel like running out? Have you ever looked at another couple and thought, "I wish our marriage was like theirs." Well, guess what! They have lots of problems too! All marriages, good, bad, and mediocre have problems! Some major, some minor, but we've got 'em! Also, we all have fights, feuds, and fusses. The only two couples I have ever met in thirty years who said they had never feuded were divorced less than a year later. Some couples aren't honest with their feelings and don't communicate; therefore, they do not face their problems and even deny them. So we must realize that problems and conflict will be a part of any serious relationship and very definitely a normal part of a "normal" marriage. I know not one couple who have even close to an "ideal" blissful romantic love feast throughout their marriage.

I must interject here that although all couples "fight," no physical violence is ever excusable. Physical, emotional and verbal abuse are all weapons never to be used in our conflicts. Why?? Because these can inflict permanent wounds that will scar your relationship until you are both so senile you forget even your own name and sex. Also, don't ever forget that when you pledged yourselves to each other, you vowed for richer or for poorer, for better or for worse, in sickness and in health. Commitment means we must solve problems. We know that we will have some bad times with some good times. Millions of married couples forget this and go for divorce far too quickly when their problems really were quite solvable or at least manageable.

Since we can now admit we all have problems, we can let down our guard, relax and open up. So, it's your choice—double your trouble or double your pleasure? Let's get on with the resolutions and solutions.

1. What can I do if I'm too close to physical violence?

2. If my spouse abuses me physically less than once a month should I just forget it?

"I'm not yawning – I'm trying not to gag."

Chapter 14

FUSE BLOWERS

I could list hundreds, maybe thousands of causes of conflict in a relationship. But I'm sure it is better for you to list a few areas of conflict that can really blow your fuse, and to identify the areas that are the most problematic in your marriage. Of course, you can avoid conflict if you will just follow one of my favorite rules:

The man is the king! — Not!!!

My wife Lorna agrees of course! — Not!!! Now that I'm sure you agree on this — we can begin on a more realistic note!

WHAT ARE SOME OF THE
MOST COMMON AREAS OF CONFLICT IN MARRIAGES?

1) **Children:**
   Discipline: too harsh, too soft.
   Times of illness.
   School problems.
   Activities: What, when, why, and where?
   Care: Who's responsible, for what?
   Creators of stress– but great rewards and good times
      also.
   Blended Families – special difficulties and
      opportunities.

But don't forget, no children means no grandchildren – Ah, there's the catch!

71

2) Finances: Always hard up. Bill collectors. Too tight fisted. Too loose. No budgets. This area will be discussed in greater detail in chapter seventeen.

3) In Laws and Out laws — Relatives and Friends: It seems everyone can give you a different opinion in any of your conflicts. Also, sometimes well meaning relatives or friends can actually compound your crisis by mis-intervention. i.e. How would you respond to your mother-in-law coming to visit for ten years?

4) Work: Never working, lazy. Always working, never has time for family. If the husband is the sole "bread winner," problems can result from his being exhausted when he comes home, while his wife is stir crazy from working at home all day. If both husband and wife have outside jobs, it is easy to fall into the trap of not having enough time for each other or for the children. Also, a two career home has unique stresses, and a competitive atmosphere may result.

5) Diverging interests: No common goals. Educational differences. Few common friends. Hobbies. Playtime activities.

Example: Hubby wants to be a couch potato and watch sports at night and all weekend while wife wants to expand her horizons and knowledge by reading.

6) Communication: Lack of. Inappropriate. Too many negatives. Not enough communication pleasantries. No "I love you's." (See chapter twenty-two.)

7) Conflict of desires and wants: conflict of egos and careers.

8) Conflicts over control: Who's the boss? Who wins the fights? If one of you controls 90% of the marriage, the other is being suppressed or squelched. You've heard of a 50/50 marriage? Many counselors advise a 30/70 relationship with each of you settling for the 30%. Get the point? If not, write this on the blackboard (or your computer) 100 times!

$$30/70 = ME\ 30\ /\ Mate\ 70$$

If you both understand and try to follow this axiom with each of you only getting your way 30% of the time, your marriage will likely be closer to 50/50!

One more quick word of advice: Throw away your tape of "I Did It My Way!"

9) Sex: Not enough, too much, boring, too pushy.

10) Infidelity: The real heart breaker. Jealousy, justified or not? Infidelity is a never-never, no-no, don't-don't, not-not.

11) Male-Female differences: There are several excellent tapes and books on this subject that I would encourage you to get. I will briefly mention that God has created us to be equal but different in many ways: sexually, relationally, emotionally, physically, and even in the way we see and think about many issues of life and family. Due to testosterone influence in fetal development, men have less cross over neurological networks from the left to the right brain hemispheres which tend to make men more focused and abstract, and women more sensitive, relational, and whole picture oriented.

Gary Smalley's video, *Hidden Keys To Loving Relationships*, illustrates this superbly! I encourage you to see it. You will laugh while gaining insight with each other in areas of discovery and mystery in which you previously never had a clue! As Gary says, "How can we men 'get with the program' if we don't even know what the program is!"

12) Personality differences: I strongly plead with you to study tapes and books by Gary Smalley and Florence Littauer on this subject. They will change your life and your relationships as you learn to understand and accept your spouse, your children, your parents, and your friends by knowing that God made each one of us as unique, different, and yes, even exciting individuals. So if I have a "Lion" personality, my wife has more "Golden Retriever," my son is a "Beaver," and my daughter an "Otter" by God's design, we can increasingly enjoy each others differences, and value one another so much more as we see the good traits in each type and blend of personality more than we see the "baddies."

1. What are some of the differences (besides anatomical) between men and women?

2. Why does it help to know that my son is a "melancholy" (Beaver) and my daughter a "sanguine" (Otter)?

3. How can we use the new information about the differences in brain pathways in men and women to our advantage in our relationships?

"A man followed you home? – *Why?*"

Chapter 15

AMBIVALENCE — AMBI-WHO?

*C*an you dislike your husband and still love him? If you are really in love, does this mean you always will feel "in love" and will get a thrill every time you see or touch each other? Are doubts possible with "true love?" Of course. In the 1970's T.V. series *All In The Family*, the Bunkers had a great episode that illustrated this extremely common occurrence. Gloria woke up one morning after six months of marriage to the great "meat head" Mike, and thought, "Who is this stranger with the messy hair, B.O., and halitosis? What have I done? I must have married the wrong person. Where's Prince Valiant?" Ambivalence is this phenomenon which occurs in all close relationships. Ambivalence means having different and sometimes opposite feelings simultaneously. (love/hate)

If you are unprepared for these feelings, they can frighten and discourage you, perhaps even threaten your marriage. But if we understand these normal, opposite feelings about our mate, we can be less disturbed by and more tolerant of some of our own feelings and some of the traits of our mate. You truly can dislike and love your mate at the same time. These insecure, angry, or bored feelings will usually pass if we so allow.

Sometimes you may feel like you despise him and wonder why you married the big creep, and other times you'll feel lovingly and strongly attracted to him and realize you did make a good choice.

Also, some of his/her good traits can have a bad side to them, making you feel ambivalent about him/her and the "good traits." Let me illustrate:

Plus Traits	Same Traits To Extreme
Good conversationalist	Talks incessantly
Good listener	Never talks or responds
Good looking (The author!)	Excessively vain about appearance
Friendly	Too friendly to other women or men
Good housekeeper	Compulsive, can't stand anything out of place
Relaxed, laid back	Lazy, slow, no initiative
Knowledgeable	Smug, know it all
Decisive	Controlling
Confident	Ego-maniac, conceited
Sexy	With everyone else
Good cook	Excessive weight gain
Good parent	Ignores spouse
Helps around the house	Breaks everything when helping

So, we do need to learn to accept the good with the bad, the pluses and the minuses, and dedicate ourselves to working hard at loving each other better and more constantly, both in words and actions.

A man who loves his wife loves himself.

Ephesians 5:28 (and Vice Versa!)

1. Can you list other good traits that to extreme can be hard to deal with or even annoying and/or obnoxious.

2. If my negative emotions begin to overcome my positive feelings toward my spouse, what should I do?

"A man like Elmo happens once in a lifetime.
But why in *my* lifetime?"

Chapter 16

LET THE HEALING BEGIN

*O*kay! Where can we start? When we have a real problem in our marriage that is creating unhappiness or dissatisfaction between us, what can we do about it? No matter what the problem is, some solution is available if we are willing to search together. It may not always be the answer we want, but the anger and direct conflict can be resolved.

How do we begin the healing of the open wound?

1) Recognize what the problem is and what caused it. How can you find the answer if you don't know the question?

2) Be willing to discuss the problem. No sulking — (Well, maybe just for 5 minutes!)

3) Be open minded. (Husbands are great at this — Not!)

4) Be calm. Over-reaction triggers over re-reaction.

5) Be willing to listen. Men remove your earplugs.

6) Realize we nearly always think we are right in the conflict, and our mate thinks he or she is right, too, or there wouldn't be a conflict. So there must be some right in both of you! Think about this. Remember this one well! Did the "Yankees" think they were right? Did the "Confederates?"

81

7) Be willing to compromise! Look for common ground you can agree on. You can both be winners in a compromise! How many battles could have been avoided? How many divorces? Can you believe Charles and Diana?

8) Make clear (write it down) your agreements, solutions, and guidelines so that this argument or problem doesn't have to be rehashed over and over. Try to solve the problem permanently.

9) Ask God for help. If you are too angry to pray together, begin praying separately, asking God to calm you and give you wisdom and understanding.

1. How do we go about finding a compromise to a very tough dispute?

2. Is it really true that when we disagree or "fight" we both have some validity to our viewpoints?

3. How can God really help you solve your problems? List some ways.

ACT V

Money Can be Fun

Chapter 17

FOR RICHER OR POORER

*O*K, OK, so we took this pledge but did we mean it? Probably none of us knew how easy it was to get poorer and how hard to achieve riches, (at least in material terms).

Most of us 5, 10, or 20 years later find that our early plans of a dream house, 2 new cars, 3 well behaved, 4 well dressed children, 5 diamond rings, and a partridge in a pear tree will probably never be realized. Sorry all you partridge pear tree fans.

Now, many of us have been through or are now experiencing serious financial problems. Of course, this doesn't affect our marriage relationship does it? You bet your booty it does! (That's a medical term; so it's allowed.) Actually, many experts in marriage counseling proclaim that money (lack of it) is the most frequent cause of strife between spouses, commonly even resulting in divorce. Most surveys put financial problems in the top two on the list for causes of breakups.

Why do so many of us get into trouble financially? Most of us are not on welfare, have a good job, (maybe 2), know how to add and subtract, and realize that we ought to live "within our means." But we don't. We buy new cars, go out to eat several times a week, borrow to buy things we think we need desperately, take our credit card to the mall, etc. Before very long we spend more than we make each month and are paying so much interest we can't pay down the debt. Then tension builds between us. Anger surfaces.

Collection agencies call. Our dentist and doctor can't see us anymore. The roof leaks, and all we can afford to eat is corn flakes and grasshopper stew. What a mess! How did it get this way?

By LACKA! — Lackawanna
Lackaknowledge
Lackadiscipline
Lackabudgeting
Lackasense and cents

Is it hopeless? Too late? Can you retrain yourselves and stop your bad habits and spending addictions????? YES! YES! YES! You can even build considerable wealth if you apply the principles in the next four chapters.

1. Why are money problems the cause of so many marriage problems? As the old saying goes, "It's only money!"

2. Is "fast food" expensive? Compare costs to sandwiches at home.

3. Why not buy a brand new car every four years?

"Of course I have high principle.
I wouldn't even think of marrying Elmo for his
money if there was another way of getting it."

Chapter 18

INSTANT RICHES
REAL RICHES

Maybe you don't realize it but in most ways you already are very rich indeed. You are living in the wealthiest country in the history of the world, in the best economics era we have ever seen, and you yourselves probably have more material wealth than at least 50% of your fellow Americans. You have many more comforts now than the kings of England and the caesars of Rome had in their day. The castles were cold. They had no indoor water or electricity, no stereos or TV, no cars or even bicycles, no soap or deodorants, and if you contracted pneumonia you died (no medicines). Also you should see King Henry's "indoor toilets!"

So here we are living far better than the kings and queens of recent history, feeling oppressed and inferior to our richer neighbors, wallowing in self pity, and yelling at each other because we have gotten ourselves into a money crunch. Of course, we men know that the bulk of the blame falls to our wives for wild spending and frivolous living. RIGHT? HA!

Well, wake up. Open your eyes, groundhogs. It's time we realized how wealthy we are already. How many things that you already possess can you think of in two minutes that you wouldn't trade for a million bucks?

HOW ARE YOU RICH NOW?

1) Money: You now are wealthier than 98% of the rest of the world's people.

91

2) Health: What would you take for your sight, hearing, legs, arms, kidneys, liver, lungs, heart? $1,000,000?? (Of course, some of us could sell 20 pounds and never miss them.)

3) Family: Would you sell a kid? Maybe you feel like it at times, but not really. As a grandpa (Papa Jon) I can say that great kids and grandkids are a treasure I wouldn't take $10,000,000 for !!

4) Friends: What an asset. (There might be a few you would sell cheap!)

5) Shelter: Millions sleep on the street. (Even when Lorna gets angry with me I still get a couch!)

6) Food: We have too much. ONE BILLION people in the world today would *sell their legs or eyes* for enough food for their family for life. *And we in America spend more on diet programs than on all our aid to the starving in our world!*

7) Freedom: If you ever forget how wonderful our freedoms are, travel to Haiti, China, Iraq, Iran, Syria, Mongolia, or dozens of other countries and count your blessings! Freedom of religion, speech, movement, thought, job selection, etc., are great treasures that we often take for granted.

8) What can you add?

We really are fortunate, aren't we? We all have problems. We all could stand a little more money, but we certainly should be very, very grateful to God for all that we have.

Now we turn to ways of finding a little more money. How to get richer. How to pay debts and build wealth. Can you do it? You Bet!

1. How are you wealthy? Count the ways!

2. On the way to building more financial independence, am I also supposed to alleviate the suffering of others, or can I wait until I really have it made?

Chapter 19

FINDING TREASURES

1) Get your priorities straight.

2) Be health conscious. Take good care of your body. God loaned you that shell to house your eternal soul for a few years. Since God created it, let's take care of it!

a.) Exercise. Your body was designed for activity.

b.) Watch diet. Less sugar, fats, alcohol, salt, coffee and red meat.

c.) Don't smoke. Smoking robs you of a hundred thousand dollars or more and fifteen years of your life. It is the most expensive, deadly habit you can acquire.

d.) Get checkups periodically. Breast exams, blood count, blood pressure, blood sugar, urine test)

e.) Learn how to relax. Breathe deeply, sleep well, get control over your worries.

3) Become more aware of what we already have now. What do you have today to be happy about? What are the most important things in your life? Who are the most important people to you? (Hint — spouse and children) Are people more important than things? What does that tell you? How about the most important being in any of our lives? Is God the central focus? If not, maybe you're wasting a perfectly good life with no real purpose and with a rotten finale! However, with God at the core of your being, you are already rich beyond your wildest dreams. You become the heir to the only true king eternally. What would you trade for happiness forever? C, UR2BNV'D (Secret Code).

4) Enjoy each day more. Take one day at a time. Smell the roses. Slow down. Take plenty of small breaks. Work hard but not too hard.

Pearl: Life is short. Make the most of yours.

5) Enjoy family more. You won't have your kids with you for very long! Enjoy them while you can. Spend time with them. Tell them you love them and are glad they are your kids.

6) Develop a better husband wife relationship. Work out your problems. Enjoy each other. Take time out together — just the two of you. Treat her to a dinner out and this time you buy! Bring home flowers (even if you have to pick them from your neighbors' rose bushes) Having a good and fun marriage adds great richness to life.

7) Develop richer friendships. (Find richer friends? No! Be a better friend.) Be interested in others. Compliment more. Be more thoughtful, dependable, and supportive.

8) Love better. Love makes life worthwhile. Love more and receive more love in return. Feel more worthwhile. Love feelings both given and received are good for body, mind, and soul.

GOD IS LOVE! See how important love is?

9) Splurge occasionally. It makes me feel special if I dine out or if I buy a new shirt occasionally. Once a year I even order tea @ 75 cents a glass at a restaurant (Last of the Big Spenders). Go to Europe once in a life time. (Maybe twice!) As Forrest Gump said: "Do not buy stuff you cannot afford — unless you really want to!"

10) Deepen your spiritual life. *The only true wealth is that which lasts. (Matthew: 6:20)* Eternal riches are promised by God for those who serve Him. As we increase our commitment to God and nurture our spiritual gifts, and as we give more love to those around us and to our Creator, we cash in on more riches in daily life even as we build more eternal riches to spend with God forever.

WE CERTAINLY ARE RICH, aren't we? And we can all become even richer as we incorporate these ten principles into our very being.

1. Why does the author say friends are true riches?

2. Do you really believe any wealth exists without God? What happens to it when you "hang it up?" Who owns everything anyhow?

3. What's wrong with good old-fashioned selfishness??

Chapter 20

MILLIONAIRE$ CAN BE FUN

*I*f you could save three dollars per day and then invest it in a tax deferred plan at ten percent for 44 years, how much would you have at retirement? $50,000? $100,000? $250,000? $500,000? $1,000,000?

Yes, One Million Dollars!

Of course, you can't cut back to save a huge three dollars daily, and nobody can invest at ten percent annually. Right?? WRONG!!! Almost anyone in America can be a millionaire. Many mutual funds, annuities, etc. yield ten percent or more annually over an extended period and probably anyone can save three dollars per day. So it is really not that hard, and doesn't take too much sacrifice or a spartan miserly lifestyle to become wealthy. Just think how many of you can save six or even ten dollars per day.

WOW!

U2R2BA Millionaire!

Study the next chapter and add your own ideas.

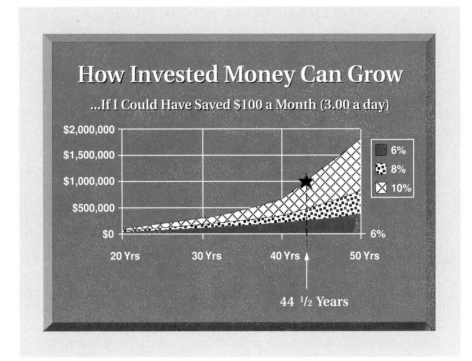

1. Can you really save 3–10 dollars a day? How?

2. Do you see any importance in understanding money and the way it multiplies as we save, or how debt explodes as we deficit spend?

"Elmo is always giving me things…He's given me gastritis,
throbbing headaches, insomnia and depression."

Chapter 21

GAIN WITHOUT PAIN

*Y*es, you can save one, two, five, maybe 10 thousand dollars a year. Here is the way.

1) Smoking: Stop. Save your health and save three dollars a day or more! If you don't smoke, start for three days, then quit and save $3.00 a day! A little humor there. (Very little!)

2) Alcohol: Stop, and save three dollars a day or more.

3) Restaurant and Fast Foods: Decrease and save at least three dollars per day

4) Food costs: Buy in larger quantities when on sale. Save Five Dollars A Day!

   • Decrease microwave food and pre-prepared foods.
   • Decrease red meats.
   • Detergent—40 pounds of generic $10.
   • Buy seasonal foods in season only.
   • Use coupons.
   • Buy less junk food and pop and impulse purchases.
   • Spend less time at the supermarket.
   • Eat more cereal and vegetables.

5) Cosmetics: Use generic products. Avoid wrinkle creams, cellulite and thigh reducing ointments, breast enlarging creams, and hair restoration products. It's junk. The promoters often lie or greatly distort the truth! Good moisturizers and makeup can be found inexpensively.

103

6) Vitamins and medication: Buy generic brands. Be sure to push your doctor about this. Example: Amoxicillin $7.00. Well known brand-name alternative $70.00. Aspirin $3.00 for 300, or brand-name Ibuprofen, $41.00 for 300.

7) Chiropractors: Seldom needed. Instead use heat, aspirin, and a back rub which will save you big bucks. A true back strain takes four to six weeks to heal with or without treatment, and spinal misalignment is rare!

8) Doctors: Select a good family practice specialist. Avoid emergency room visits unless it is a true emergency. Feel free to ask your doctor questions about necessity of surgery, x-rays, lab medicines, etc. For a cold or a minor rash, stay home and save 50 bucks.

9) Dentists: Select a good generalist. Ask about the true need of x-rays and other procedures.

10) Insurance: Don't overbuy. Deductible policies are good. Shop around. HMO's can save a lot. Only protect what you can't afford to lose.

11) Cars: Don't buy new until you can afford to throw away at least $5,000. (This is due to $ depreciation, $ taxes, $ interest, and $ insurance costs.)

Car #1: good 1–3 year old with low mileage.
Car #2: Cheapo utility vehicle — liability insurance only.

12) Utility bills: Automatic light "turner-offers." During the summer months set your thermostat at 78 degrees and buy a fan or two to keep cool. During the winter months set your thermostat at 68 degrees and wear a sweater.

13) Phone bills: Call long distance at low rate times (Saturdays or evenings). Cancel call waiting and other unnecessary options.

14) House: Don't buy a house when you are first married. Don't put in a swimming pool or renovate extensively. Later, buy a house that needs some touch ups. Then you can buy or build your "dream house" at your 25th anniversary when you can truly afford it.

15) Clothes and shoes: Buy them on sale only. Forget labels, fads, designer clothes, etc. Learn how to sew up minor tears, etc. Buy the next larger size for young children.

16) Jewelry: Not an investment. Buy at 60 to 75% off and don't watch shopping channels very often!

17) Divorces: Don't. It's too expensive! Love your spouse and try to work out your problems. Work on learning to have fun together again.

18) CD's and tapes: Don't overbuy and always buy on sale. Who cares if you don't have the latest rock or country and western hit? Sing it yourself instead.

19) Movies: Buy $1.50 tickets at matinees or rent $1.00 videos. Get basic cable and maybe one movie channel.

20) Vacations: Take some, but don't blow money on expensive hotels or fancy-schmancy restaurants. Don't buy a 2nd home until you are a millionaire. Watch out for "time share" schemes.

21) Furniture: TVs, Stereos, VCRs, etc. Buy on sale and don't impulse buy. Shop around.

22) Boats: Rent. Don't buy.

23) Education: Get one. Opens many doors.

24) Drugs: Don't be crazy.

25) Car repairs: Find a good mechanic with low overhead.

26) Prevention: Avoid accidents. Drive safely, no tickets. Install smoke alarms, night lights, gates on stairs, locks on pool gate. Put dangerous items out of the reach of small children.

27) Children: Have the number you want and then protect from "surprises." Don't overspend on toys, clothes, etc. too often. Let Grandma do it!

28) Credit Cards: Throw away or pay full balance each month (16–21% interest) No installment plans. If you can't pay cash, don't buy it! (Make only rare exceptions to this rule.)

29) Work: Get a good job. Proverbs 28:19 says: "Hard work brings prosperity. Playing around brings poverty."

30) Avoid Health food fads. Diet plans are expensive. Avoid TV and mail promos, "free" vacation ads, phone solicitations, and other such scams. FRAUDS = 30 Billion dollars a year!

There is **NO FREE LUNCH**! Real estate "opportunities" and other get rich quick schemes are usually RIP-OFFS! *Proverbs 28:22* says: *"Trying to get rich quick is evil and leads to poverty."*

So, learn to save and invest carefully and wisely. Then enjoy financial security. After all, you've earned it!

1. Go over this list carefully and add to it. You probably can save thousands more per year than you thought.

2. Can I get too obsessed with saving to the point of being a "Scrooge?"

So, now that you are going to ease your financial pressures, you'll have a lot more energy to use on the next vital topic.

ACT VI

Communication Can be Fun

"You haven't talked to me for a week,
and I can't thank you enough."

Chapter 22

CAN WE TALK?

Pearl: You can't know anyone unless you communicate with him/her. You can't really love anyone you don't know. Therefore, decreased communication directly results in decreased love (and vice versa).

"Can we talk? We talk about everything. He is such an interesting man to be with and a great listener too!"

"She is so much fun, never at a loss for words. We talk and laugh all the time together!"

Healthy premarital intercourse is non-sexual. It is dialogue/communication. Almost all couples I interview before marriage say that their communication flows freely, but two years after marriage, a large percentage of these same couples say communication has become obstructed. What happens to so many couples that causes a blockage of this extremely vital "link of love"? Why can't we talk anymore? WHAT CAUSES CONSTIPATED COMMUNICATION?

Of course there are many factors and causes, and I will start your thinking by listing just a few:

1) **Lack of effort:** It is very easy to fall into a rut and to sit in front of the TV like a zombie. Besides what can you talk about after two years that hasn't been said already? It does take effort to talk sometimes, but so does eating, walking, and driving a car. How far would we get each day without making an effort to do these tasks? Just being aware of the need to communicate more and better can stimulate us to think of many things to discuss. Turning off the TV for a week might be the first step.

After thirty-six years of marriage, Lorna and I still uncover new "secrets" about each other by exploring our past, present, and future together. Lorna just told me last week how she felt about a cute guy in her high school who seemed to ignore her, but this past summer he told her that he had always thought her unattainable. Lucky for her she never knew that and married me instead, huh? Of course it wouldn't have changed anything, since when she met me, all other "challengers" didn't have a chance! She'll never find out that I once paid 50 bucks for a Charles Atlas muscle building course that turned me from a 100 pound weakling into a 200 pound superman!

Well, putting foolishness aside for a second, let's get back to the future. Make the effort to discover new things to talk about. If necessary, force yourself to be interested.

2) **Lack of Knowledge:** Many, perhaps most couples don't have a clue about how to properly use the multiple methods of communication. We muddle along through life and marriage never caring enough to learn more effective ways of expression. We get into stupid, unnecessary arguments that are caused by lack of forethought, by inappropriate words, by generalizations that are untrue, etc. Words like "always" and "never" should never be used in arguments. Also, we all could learn to smile more at our spouses. Body language, facial expression, and voice tones can be consciously changed to give a more relaxed, less confrontational appearance when we are discussing both minor and major issues. Can we learn more and better techniques? You bet! Read the next chapter twice!

3) Hostility: Unresolved anger leads to bitterness and hostility and will block good communication between you until the source is uncovered and openly discussed. Why is saying "I'm sorry" so hard? Why do we always have to be "right"? Can you ask for forgiveness? Can you forgive? Don't let hostile feelings smolder until resentments set in. This can stifle communication and kill a marriage!

4) Fear of getting close: Some of us were reared in a stuffy, cold family environment that makes it difficult for us to be warm towards anyone, including our own family. Also some of us have been deeply hurt by others and have become too skeptical and afraid of rejection; so we keep our guard up at all times. This obviously impairs our relationships. But we can learn to be warmer and more relaxed with people. We can consciously make the effort to be more trusting, less suspicious, less fearful, and more expressive.

Pearl: Limited communication equals limited love!

5) Lack of acceptance: True love is unconditional. Love means acceptance of the way you are. You don't have to change before I can love you. I respect you and what you have to say. If I don't feel accepted by you, can I really communicate with you?

These then are some of the blocks to effective communication. The quicker we DE-SCOVER, DE-SCUSS, and DE-FUSE these explosive boobytraps of communication, the quicker we can DE-STROY them.

1. Why do we have to talk after work? I'm tired.

2. How about my "space." Do I need time for myself too?

3. Is mumbling, "yeah, no, maybe, and uh huh," enough to qualify as a good communicator?

4. How can I open the lines of communication with my spouse?

Chapter 23

FOR BETTER OR BEST – THE TRUE "EXPRESSO"

I know you think you understand
what you believe I said,
but I'm not sure you realize that
what you heard is not what I meant!

"I hate your guts, you slimy piece of dinosaur dodo!" Now that's expressiveness! Effective, but dangerous, and definitely will escalate the scale of confrontation. There must be a better way to reveal anger that is less threatening to your spouse and to your relationship. Maybe the "creep" did treat you mean. But perhaps he is totally oblivious to the injury he caused you. Selecting the appropriate words, using the skills of moderation, controlled emotion, and calm discussion can avoid massive blow-ups in any relationship.

*A soft answer turns away wrath
but a harsh word arouses anger.*

Proverbs 15:1

But most of us just aren't aware of the many tools of expression that we can use so much more alertly and tactfully than we now do.

To begin with, I think the old but new concept of WORD PICTURES is very much under used. It is so helpful to parallel our feelings to an object as we try to help our mate and our children understand what we are trying to say.

Example:

"When you leave in the morning without kissing me goodby, I feel like I have been abandoned in a desert."

"When you throw cold food on my plate, I think I am back in the army in Fort Avalanche, Alaska."

115

"How can you say I don't talk to you?
Didn't I just tell you to shut your big mouth?"

"When you come to bed without a bath, it takes me back to my childhood farm days cleaning the pig pen and slopping the hogs."

"When you scream at me so angrily I feel like I have been attacked by an enraged lion."

"Last night you hugged me spontaneously, and I want you to know that it made me feel like Cinderella in the arms of her prince."

"When we fight, it seems like two pit bulls going for the throat."

So, all of us can still learn more about the many ways of communication and how to use them more effectively. Let me list a few:

1. Words: The most obvious but often the most misused. How often do we say things we don't mean because we use the wrong words? How many fights begin because we don't express ourselves clearly? Also, can we learn to be more courteous and kind in our expressions to the most important person in our lives? (hint—YOUR SPOUSE)

2. Silence: Very effective in showing anger but if prolonged, very hurtful.

3. Voice inflections: Tense high pitched tones can create an angry response. A pleasant tone with bright upturns can create a happy atmosphere.

4. Eyes: They speak volumes. Examples: rolled up, shut, soft, sexy, narrow slits, absent stares, crossed.

5. Outward emotion: Crying, blushing, anger.

6. Facial expressions: Smiles, frowns, puckers, snarls, yawns, relaxed. Do we need to smile more with our spouse and children? 99.999% of us do!!

7. Body language: Agitated, tense, relaxed, sexy, sloppy, wimpy, self confident. All of these are reflected by how we stand, sit, walk, etc.

8. Touch: Most of us don't use this vital method of communication nearly enough. Hugs are great. A research study found we each need about a dozen a day, and we get or give only about one or two per day. Newborns actually can quit eating and die without touch. We all must learn to use touching more often and effectively. A playful pat on his rear can lead to a mountain-top experience of discourse and other-course!

9. Writing cards: Love letters (after 20 years?) Notes on pillows or hidden in pockets can be fun and very romantic. One sweet note Lorna left under my pillow said, "Once a king always a king, but once a knight is enough!"

10. Thoughtful actions: Flowers, helping with household chores, surprises, etc. Can you think of more?

11. Laughter: "The family who prays together stays together" is a very wise old quotation, and I would insert the word laughs as another axiom.

We all use these ways of communicating, but how appropriately? Most of us could use the last four a lot more often! Now, are you ready to listen?

1. Why are written notes and cards important?

2. Show why touching is a vital way of communicating.

3. Can you remember examples of times when you hurt your spouse's feelings by using a word inappropriately or by sounding tense or harsh because you were upset about work or the kids, etc.?

"Believe me, its not *my* face
I'm hiding behind the paper."

Chapter 24

HUH???

J have asked my gorgeous wife to write this chapter because she is much better than I am at putting this subject into practice. I am finally learning to listen. I'm really trying. In fact lots of people say I am very trying. It's just that I have so much to say! Lorna—tell 'em!

OK, Jon, here goes. Are you listening? And don't say "Huh?"

Let everyone be quick to listen, slow to talk, slow to get angry.
James 1:19.

"Jon, did you hear me?"

"Huh? Oh yeah, yeah I heard you."

"Yes, but did you listen?"

"What do you mean, listen?"

"Did you listen closely enough so that you really heard what I said?"

"Yeah. Huh?"

How many times have you felt the same way about your spouse's listening ability? It's not uncommon for couples to hear but not to listen. The dictionary defines "listen" as "attend closely for the purpose of hearing; pay attention." Do we listen to each other ? Do we just hear sounds or do we concentrate on what our spouse is saying? If we listen closely, we can hear our spouse expressing desires. Do we pick up on them and carry through or do we ignore them?

"I wish you would spend more time at home."

"I wish you'd wear that outfit more often."

"I wish the house weren't so messy when I get home."

"I wish you would help me with the children more."

"I get tired of the TV being on all of the time."

LISTEN. If we don't pick up on suggestions, our spouse will feel like he/she is not important to us. Then it will be easy for resentments to build. Listening is a loving action. If you must, force yourself to listen. Set aside a few minutes each day to listen to each others feeling and concerns.

Some points to remember:

1) **Maintain good eye contact.** Rolling your eyes, staring out the window or at the floor, reading the newspaper, watching TV frequently, looking at the clock. These all say "You're not important to me."

2) **Your posture speaks volumes.** Crossing your arms or slouching indicates boredom and irritation.

3) **Don't interrupt.** You'll get your turn.

4) **Ask questions to show interest.**

5) **Quickly offering advice or scolding are sure "turn offs."**

Examples:

"If you'd unplug the telephone you'd have more time."

"This is what you should do."

"You shouldn't feel that way."

So squelch the urge to give advice or to lecture.

The following from an unknown source sums it up well:

Listen

When I ask you to listen to me and you start giving advice you have not done what I asked.

When I ask you to listen to me and you begin to tell me why I shouldn't feel that way, you are trampling on my feelings. When I ask you to listen to me and you feel you have to do something to solve my problem, you have failed me, strange as that may seem.

So please listen and just hear me.

And, if you want to talk, wait a minute for your turn and I'll listen to you.

Remember: "Talking is sharing. Listening is caring."

Pearl: God made us with two ears, but only one mouth! Can we listen twice as much as we speak?

Take a tip from nature . . .
Your ears aren't made to shut, but your mouth is.

Take a tip from scripture, *Proverbs 13:3.*
Self control means controlling the tongue! A quick retort can ruin everything.

"Big deal; ok so the cat ate your homemade cobbler.
I'll get you another cat."

Chapter 25

TALL WALLS MUST FALL
COMMUNION FOR UNION

*I*n this fourth and last chapter on communication I will give you fifteen magic keys that will unlock the doors to your secret closets and open the barriers to the close relationship you both want and deserve. Since communication is such a vital part of marriage, family, and all other relationships in your life, the more you use these keys the better life itself can be. So let's get knocking down them blocks!

PRINCIPLES TO BETTER COMMUNICATION

1. Learn to use the different ways of communicating and use them appropriately. Quit frowning so much. Smile LOTS! Touch more. Give hugs. Be more thoughtful. Sing more. Write more love notes.

2. Be sure that you know that communication is an exchange, a two way dialogue. That means equal time of giving and receiving.

3. Be interested in others. Be interesting by being interested! The biggest bores are those who are interested only in themselves!

4. Learn to Listen! Be attentive. By listening you are saying, "You are important to me." Be an active listener.

5. Be Tactful. Communication can be closed if unnecessary anger is displayed. Unnecessary anger causes defensiveness in the other person. Many friendships are hurt this way needlessly. Choose the words you use carefully when tackling a problem or addressing a sensitive issue.

6. Be Accepting of the other person as a equal. Respect his or her opinion. Speak softly. Listen. Don't interrupt. Don't try to be right. Learn how to say, "I was wrrrrro. I was wrrroooooooon... I was wwwrrrroooonnnn... I may have been mistaken!" You are not always right. Nobody is always right. Be tolerant of differences. Be non-judgmental.

7. Be available. Communication stops if you're too busy to pay attention to what your spouse is trying to say to you.

8. Act. Don't react. Letting someone else control your emotions and actions by causing you to react in anger will stop communication.

9. Be positive, not negative. If you're always negative, critical, griping, and pessimistic, no one will want to communicate with you. I have some patients I dread to see because they are chronic complainers.

10. Say it straight. Sometimes we create a lot of trouble because we evade the real problem that is bugging us.

11. Express your feelings rather than giving judgments or sermons!

12. Check out meanings. Don't fly off the handle over a misinterpreted comment. (i.e., When he calls you an old bag, maybe he really meant to call you a young bag!)

13. Ask questions when you don't understand what is being said. Asking questions demonstrates that you really want to understand what your spouse is trying to express.

14. Be willing to compromise. Don't insist on having to prove you are right all the time. Being right can sometimes cause you more trouble than being wrong! Often compromise is the best solution to a difference in opinion. Our daughter, Teri, was reared with a Scotch pine Christmas tree tradition. Her husband, Stan, with a Douglas Fir OBSESSION. Their compromise? An artificial tree!

15. Practice communication. Talk. Smile. Talk. Talk. Talk. What should a married couple talk about? Everything!

Why should we try to overcome barriers of communication? Because without communication LOVE DIES. If I don't feel accepted by you, how can I really communicate with you?

If I can be more tender, more receptive, more interested, more tactful, more positive and less negative, and enlarge my ears and shrink my big mouth, better communication leading to more love and understanding is almost guaranteed to "miraculously" occur!

127

1. Why do I have to be tactful at home? I thought I could "let it all hang out" at home?

2. How can I develop a more positive attitude and outlook on life? I'm just naturally a negative old poophead! Can God help me, or am I hopeless?

3. What if I can't think of anything to talk about? Can't I just listen real good and grunt?

   After reading this chapter go ahead and practice good eye contact, good body language, smiles and listening ears and then see if you can communicate more effectively!

Chapter 26

IT REALLY CAN BE FUN!!!

So we've talked about true love, commitment, pitfalls, problem solving, sex and more sex, pleasing and understanding your spouse, financial matters, and commitment.

Are we serious when we say "Marriage Can Be Fun"? You bet! You may be past 30, 40, 50, or 60, but we're all still just boys and girls with a few wrinkles and less hair. Somewhere under that cool dignified facade or beneath that grouchy, old goat demeanor there hides a youthful spirit wanting to enjoy life and marriage again. So, lighten up, work hard, but play just as hard at making your marriage stronger and more rewarding to both of you. You are two intelligent young or nearly young folks who deserve and can achieve all this if you are only willing to use these new tools and change patterns of behavior in your relationship. Loving and caring, being loved and cared for, and sharing life's ups and downs are vital ingredients for a happy, meaningful life together. A happy marriage with lots of good times over the years to help us get through the rougher times is an achievable goal that we can and will reach!!

Now don't forget the order of life's priorities.
1. God
2. Spouse
3. Children
4. Others
5. Other things (job, etc.)

So, let's get on with it,

AND HAVE A GREAT TIME DOING IT!!

MARRIAGE *CAN* BE FUN!!!

AFTER LOGS

*L*ight up the fire. Learn again to snuggle. Pop some corn. "Hubbies," make a few macho sounds (woof woof). "Wife-ees" wiggle and giggle. Make sure that kids are locked in their beds, lights low, soft music . . .

Now go to it — 'Doing' what comes naturally should be the result soon if you read, reread, and re-reread this book together, apply its contents, practice most of these suggestions and turn on again to living, laughing, and loving!

Have Fun, Kids!

It's your life to be messed or blessed.

Happiness or misery together — Which are you choosing?